I know about numbers.
I can count and add.

Dick Bruna

I know
about numbers

Methuen Children's Books

1

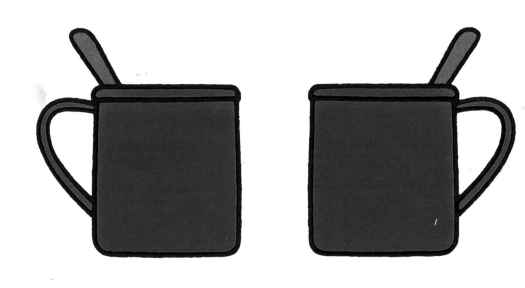

$$1+1=2$$

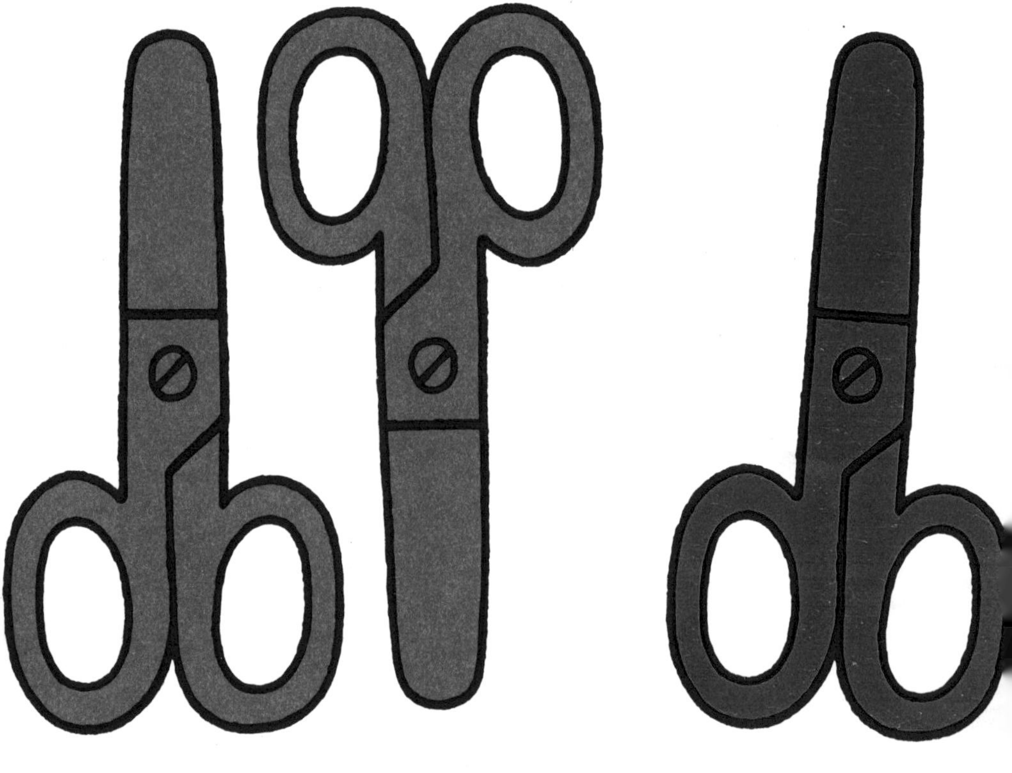

$$2 + 1 = 3$$

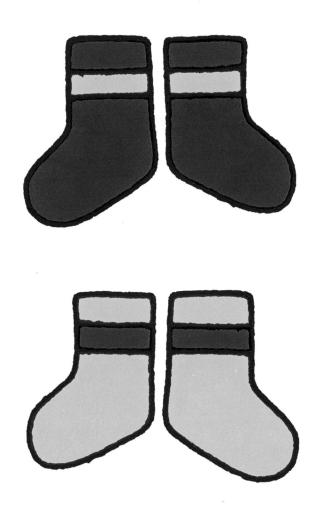

$$2+2=4$$

$$3 + 2 = 5$$

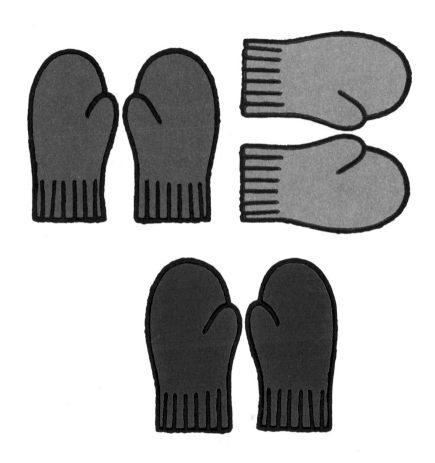

2 + 2 + 2 = 6

(that's 3 pairs of mittens)

$$4 + 3 = 7$$

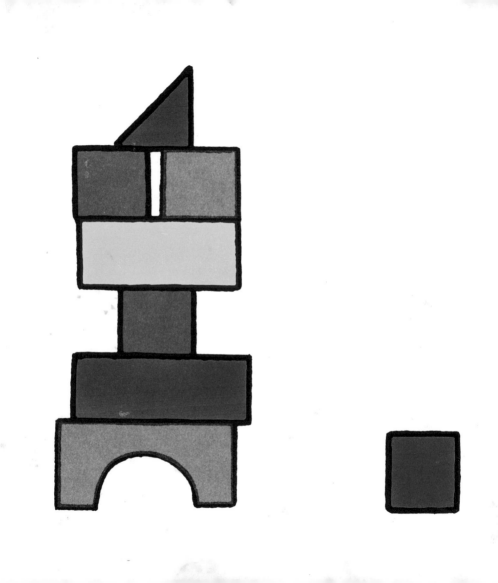

$$7+1=8$$

$$5 + 4 = 9$$

$$7 + 3 = 10$$

So, you see,
I know about numbers.